A
MONTH
of PRAYER

ST. BERNARD OF CLAIRVAUX

A
MONTH
of PRAYER

ST. BERNARD OF CLAIRVAUX

Wyatt North
BOOKS THAT INSPIRE

INTRODUCTION

Bernard of Clairvaux (1090-1153) was a Burgundian abbot who was credited with the revitalization of the Benedictine order through the nascent Order of the Cistercians. He lived during the time of schism, when the head of the church was in contention. Benedict was chosen to help decide between the claims on the papacy—ultimately siding with Pope Innocent II rather than the Antipope Anacletus II. Benedict played a significant role in unifying the church and protecting its unity against the threat that this dispute signified. For Bernard, the issue at hand was not merely a question of order and polity but a matter of loving God properly.

Saint Bernard is known chiefly from his writings on loving God. It is one thing to recognize that God *loves us*, but how is it that we, who are limited by our human capacities, can return God's love properly? Certainly, it's not a matter of degrees or a measure of love. If God loves us with all that He is—and He does—and we love Him with all that we are, our finite love cannot compare to the infinite love that God extends toward us. Nonetheless, Jesus declared that all of the law could be summed up by two commands. The greatest being that we should love the Lord with all our heart, mind, and strength. The second, of course, being that we should love our neighbors as ourselves.

DAY 1

God is love. If we are going to ask why it is important that we love God, the answer must start with God's nature and character. This is the insight that St. Bernard gave in his book, *On Loving God,* and we would do well to consider it. Often, we hear people say things like, "I couldn't love a God who allows bad things to happen," and other similar sentiments. However, God *is* love. We love because He first loved us. The cross is sufficient to demonstrate the basis of our love of God. It's there that we should look, not within the contingencies of our lives, if we are to love God properly.

Meditations from St. Bernard

You want me to tell you why God is to be loved and how much. I answer, the reason for loving God is God Himself; and the measure of love due to Him is immeasurable love. Is this plain? Doubtless, to a thoughtful man; but I am debtor to the unwise also. A word to the wise is sufficient; but I must consider simple folk too. Therefore, I set myself joyfully to explain more in detail what is meant above.

We are to love God for Himself, because of a twofold reason; nothing is more reasonable, nothing more profitable. When one asks, Why should I love God? he may mean, What is lovely in God? or What shall I gain by loving God? In either case, the same sufficient cause of love exists, namely, God Himself.

And first, of His title to our love. Could any title be greater than this, that He gave Himself for us unworthy wretches? And being God, what better gift could He offer than Himself? Hence, if one seeks for God's claim upon our love here is the chiefest: Because He first loved us (I John 4.19).

Ought He not to be loved in return, when we think who loved, whom He loved, and how much He loved? For who is He that loved? The same of whom every spirit testifies: 'Thou art my God: my goods are nothing unto Thee' (Ps. 16.2, Vulg.). And is not His love that wonderful charity which 'seeketh not her own'? (I Cor.13.5). But for whom was such unutterable love made manifest? The apostle tells us: 'When we were enemies, we were reconciled to God by the death of His Son' (Rom. 5.10). So it was God who loved us, loved us freely, and loved us while yet we were enemies. And how great was this love of His? St. John answers: 'God so loved the world that He gave His only-begotten Son, that whosoever believeth in Him should not perish, but have everlasting life' (John 3.16). St. Paul adds: 'He spared not His own Son, but delivered Him up for us all' (Rom. 8.32); and the Son says of Himself, 'Greater love hath no man than this, that a man lay down his life for his friends' (John 15.13).

St. Bernard of
Clairvaux. *On Loving
God*, Ch. 1.

Additional Biblical Reflections: Deuteronomy 6:5; John 14:21; Galatians 2:20.

Prayer

Lord, your love for us is greater than we can possibly comprehend. Yet, so often, the love we have for you pales in comparison to the love you demonstrated for us on the cross. Lord, grant us hearts that conform to the image of your Son so that we might love you as you love us. Amen.

DAY 2

Even besides the cross, the Love of God is abundant and evident to believers and unbelievers alike. Despite our lack of gratitude, God continues to grant earthly blessings like food, sunlight, and food even to those who blaspheme His name. As such, life in creation testifies to our basis of love for God on several levels. If we do not see cause to love God, it is on account of the hardness of our hearts, not on account of any lack of graciousness on God's part.

Meditations from St. Bernard

Those who admit the truth of what I have said know, I am sure, why we are bound to love God. But if unbelievers will not grant it, their ingratitude is at once confounded by His innumerable benefits, lavished on our race, and plainly discerned by the senses. Who is it that gives food to all flesh, light to every eye, air to all that breathe? It would be foolish to begin a catalogue, since I have just called them innumerable: but I name, as notable instances, food, sunlight and air; not because they are God's best gifts, but because they are essential to bodily life. Man must seek in his own higher nature for the highest gifts; and these are dignity, wisdom and virtue. By dignity I mean free-will, whereby he not only excels all other earthly creatures, but has dominion over them. Wisdom is the power whereby he recognizes this dignity, and perceives also that it is no accomplishment of his own. And virtue impels man to seek eagerly for Him who is man's Source, and to lay fast hold on Him when He has been found.

Now, these three best gifts have each a twofold character. Dignity appears not only as the prerogative of human nature, but also as the cause of that fear and dread of man which is upon every beast of the earth. Wisdom perceives this distinction, but owns that though in us, it is, like all good qualities, not of us. And lastly, virtue moves us to search eagerly for an Author, and, when we have found Him, teaches us to cling to Him yet more eagerly. Consider too that dignity without wisdom is nothing worth; and wisdom is harmful without virtue, as this argument following shows: There is no glory in having a gift without knowing it. But to know only that you have it, without knowing that it is not of yourself that you have it, means self-glorying, but no true glory in God. And so the apostle says to men in such cases, 'What hast thou that thou didst not receive? Now, if thou didst receive it, why dost thou glory as if thou hadst not received it? (I Cor. 4.7). He asks, Why dost thou glory? but goes on, as if thou hadst not received it, showing that the guilt is not in glorying over a possession, but in glorying as though it had not been received. And rightly such glorying is called vain-glory, since it has not the solid foundation of truth. The apostle shows how to discern the true glory from the false, when he says, He that glorieth, let him glory in the Lord, that is, in the Truth, since our Lord is Truth (I Cor. 1.31; John 14.6).

St. Bernard of
Clairvaux. *On Loving
God*, Ch. 2.

Additional Biblical Reflections: 1 Chronicles 29:12-13; Matthew 5:45; Philippians 4:19.

Prayer

Lord, you open your hand to satisfy the needs of every living thing. Your generosity is not contingent on our faith, but our faith is awakened by your graciousness. Grant us, likewise, such gratitude so that we might love you as we ought. In Jesus's name. Amen.

DAY 3

In today's meditation, St. Bernard tells us that if our love of God has fallen out of balance, it's often because the way we love ourselves—either loving ourselves too much or too little—is likewise out of balance. That is why we must examine ourselves in our pursuit of loving God. For, if we do not consider ourselves and our spiritual state properly, we will inevitably miss the mark when it comes to our disposition toward God.

Meditations from St. Bernard

We must know, then, what we are, and that it is not of ourselves that we are what we are. Unless we know this thoroughly, either we shall not glory at all, or our glorying will be vain. Finally, it is written, 'If thou know not, go thy way forth by the footsteps of the flock' (Cant. 1.8). And this is right. For man, being in honor, if he know not his own honor, may fitly be compared, because of such ignorance, to the beasts that perish. Not knowing himself as the creature that is distinguished from the irrational brutes by the possession of reason, he commences to be confounded with them because, ignorant of his own true glory which is within, he is led captive by his curiosity, and concerns himself with external, sensual things. So he is made to resemble the lower orders by not knowing that he has been more highly endowed than they.

We must be on our guard against this ignorance. We must not rank ourselves too low; and with still greater care we must see that we do not think of ourselves more highly than we ought to think, as happens when we foolishly impute to ourselves whatever good may be in us. But far more than either of these kinds of ignorance, we must hate and shun that presumption which would lead us to glory in goods not our own, knowing that they are not of ourselves but of God, and yet not fearing to rob God of the honor due unto Him. For mere ignorance, as in the first instance, does not glory at all; and mere wisdom, as in the second, while it has a kind of glory, yet does not glory in the Lord. In the third evil case, however, man sins not in ignorance but deliberately, usurping the glory which belongs to God. And this arrogance is a more grievous and deadly fault than the ignorance of the second, since it contemns God, while the other knows Him not. Ignorance is brutal, arrogance is devilish. Pride only, the chief of all iniquities, can make us treat gifts as if they were rightful attributes of our nature, and, while receiving benefits, rob our Benefactor of His due glory.

Wherefore to dignity and wisdom we must add virtue, the proper fruit of them both. Virtue seeks and finds Him who is the Author and Giver of all good, and who must be in all things glorified; otherwise, one who knows what is right yet fails to perform it, will be beaten with many stripes (Luke 12.47). Why? you may ask. Because he has failed to put his knowledge to good effect, but rather has imagined mischief upon his bed (PS. 36.4); like a wicked servant, he has turned aside to seize the glory which, his own knowledge assured him, belonged only to his good Lord and Master. It is plain, therefore, that dignity without wisdom is useless and that wisdom without virtue is accursed. But when one possesses virtue, then wisdom and dignity are not dangerous but blessed.

St. Bernard of
Clairvaux. *On Loving
God*, Ch. 2.

Additional Biblical Reflections: Matthew 7:5; 1 Corinthians 11:27-31; 2 Corinthians 13:5.

Prayer

Dear Lord, show us our own hearts so that we might be ever aware of our condition. If we think too highly of ourselves, curb our egos. If we think too low of ourselves, remind us that you loved us enough that you would exalt us should we cling to your son. Grant this so that we might be ever more aware of our need for you. Amen.

DAY 4

In today's meditation, in a letter he wrote to several monks, St. Bernard tells us that mercy is not something merited. It does not judge but *feels*. Christian love is a matter of the heart, not the mind. When we rationalize our decisions to love, it is rarely our neighbor whose interest is at heart. Rather, by rationalizing, we are bound to ask whether love is beneficial to the self, which, in turn, contradicts the very definition of love.

Meditations from St. Bernard

To the very dear Lord and Reverend father Guigues, Prior of the Grande Chartreuse, and to the holy brethren who are with him, Brother Bernard of Clairvaux offers his humble service.

In the first place, when lately I approached your parts, I was prevented by unfavourable circumstances from coming to see you and to make your acquaintance; and although my excuse may perhaps be satisfactory to you, I am not able, I confess, to pardon myself for missing the opportunity. It is a vexation to me that my occupations brought it about, not that I should neglect to come to see you, but that I was unable to do so. This I frequently have to endure, and therefore my anger is frequently excited. Would that I were worthy to receive the sympathy of all my kind friends. Otherwise I shall be doubly unhappy if my disappointment does not excite your pity. But I give you an opportunity, my brethren, of exercising brotherly compassion towards me, not that I merit it. Pity me not because I am worthy, but because I am poor and needy. Justice inquires into the merit of the supplicant, but mercy only looks to his unhappiness. True mercy does not judge, but feels; does not discuss the occasion which presents itself, but seizes it. When affection calls us, reason is silent. When Samuel wept over Saul it was by a feeling of pity, and not of approval (1 Samuel xv. 13). David shed tears over his parricidal son, and although they were profitless, yet they were pious. Therefore do ye pity me (because I need it, not because I merit it), ye who have obtained from God the grace to serve Him without fear, far from the tumults of the world from which ye are freed. Happy those whom He has hidden in His tabernacle in the day of evil men; they shall trust in the shadow of His wings until the iniquity be overpast. As for me, poor, unhappy, and miserable, labour is my portion. I seem to be as a little unfledged bird almost constantly out of the shelter of its nest, exposed to wind and tempest. I am troubled, and I stagger like a drunken man, and my whole conscience is gnawed with care. Pity me, then; for although I do not merit pity I need it, as I have said.

St. Bernard of
Clairvaux. *Letter to the
Monks of the Grand
Chartreuse.*

Additional Biblical Reflections: John 1:16; Ephesians 4:4-9; 1 Corinthians 12:9-10.

Prayer

Lord, mercy or pity is not something we deserve, nor is it something we should withhold on account of someone else's lack of merit. For, while we did not yet deserve it, you chose to die for our sake. Let us embrace your grace so that not only might we achieve salvation for ourselves, but by grace, we might also love others. Amen.

DAY 5

Vanity—or the love of self—we hear from St. Bernard leads us to have hatred for the truth, which also leads to our spiritual blindness. Again, we hear why we must examine ourselves properly to learn to love God properly. This is why, for instance, it was not just a judgment but an act of grace when God allowed His people, in the Scriptures, to experience exile and punishment. It was not punishment for its own sake but for the sake of killing vanity and opening hearts and minds to Him and His truth.

Meditations from St. Bernard

The love of vanity is the contempt of truth, and the contempt of truth the cause of our blindness. And because they did not like, he says, to retain God in their knowledge, He gave them over unto a reprobate mind (Rom. i. 28).

From this blindness, then, it follows that we frequently love and approve that which is not for that which is; since while we are in this body we are wandering from Him who is the Fulness of Existence. And what is man, O God, except that Thou hast taken knowledge of Him? If the knowledge of God is the cause that man is anything, the want of this makes him nothing. But He who calls those things which are not as though they were, pitying those reduced in a manner to nothing, and not yet able to contemplate in its reality, and to embrace by love that hidden manna, concerning which the Apostle says: Your life is hidden with Christ in God (Cor. iii. 3). But in the meantime He has given us to taste it by faith and to seek for by strong desire. By these two we are brought for the second time from not being, to begin to be that His (new) creature, which one day shall pass into a perfect man, into the measure of the stature of the fulness of Christ. That, without doubt, shall take place, when righteousness shall be turned into judgment, that is, faith into knowledge, the righteousness which is of faith into the righteousness of full knowledge, and also the hope of this state of exile shall be changed into the fulness of love. For if faith and love begin during the exile, knowledge and love render perfect those in the Presence of God. For as faith leads to full knowledge, so hope leads to perfect love, and, as it is said, If ye will not believe ye shall not understand (Is. vii. 9, acc. to lxx.), so it may equally be said with fitness, if you have not hoped, you will not perfectly love. Knowledge then is the fruit of faith, perfect charity of hope. In the meantime the just lives by faith (Hab. ii. 4), but he is not happy except by knowledge; and he aspires towards God as the hart desires the water-brooks; but the blessed drinks with joy from the fountain of the Saviour, that is, he delights in the fulness of love.

St. Bernard of
Clairvaux. *Letter VI.*

Additional Biblical Reflections: Habakkuk 2:4; Isaiah 7:9; Romans 1:28.

Prayer

Lord, please destroy our vanity so that we might see your truth and, thereby, see you as you are. Let us not be blind by imagining we see better than we do what is good and right, but soften our hard hearts so that we might pursue what you have told us is good and salutary. In Jesus's name. Amen.

DAY 6

Apart of loving God, St. Bernard teaches us today, is to both have knowledge of the truth and delight in it. Many people, it seems, learn the faith on a mental level. They learn the Scriptures and the canons of faith, and some even pursue academic degrees. However, many such persons have little *delight* in their knowledge; others have much delight in the truth of the faith but cannot be bothered to study the truths of God. St. Bernard urges us to maintain a balance in our love of God and the truth.

Meditations from St. Bernard

Thus understanding and love, that is, the knowledge of and delight in the truth, are, perhaps, as it were, the two arms of the soul, with which it embraces and comprehends with all saints the length and breadth, the height and depth, that is the eternity, the love, the goodness, and the wisdom of God. And what are all these but Christ? He is eternity, because "this is life eternal to know Thee the true God and Jesus Christ whom Thou hast sent" (S. John xvii. 3). He is Love, because He is God, and God is Love (1 S. John iv. 16). He is both the Goodness of God and the Wisdom of God (I Cor. i. 24), but when shall these things be? When shall we see Him as He is? For the expectation of the creature waiteth for the revelation of the sons of God. For the creature was subjected unto vanity, not willingly (Rom. viii. 19, 20). It is that vanity diffused through all which makes us desire to be praised even when we are blamable, and not to be willing to praise those whom we know to be worthy of it. But this too is vain, that we, in our ignorance, frequently praise what is not, and are silent about what is.

What shall we say to this, but that the children of men are vain, the children of men are deceitful upon the weights, so that they deceive each other by vanity (Ps. lxi. 9; lxx.). We praise falsely, and are foolishly pleased, so that they are vain who are praised, and they false who praise. Some flatter and are deceptive, others praise what they think deserving, and are deceived; others pride themselves in the commendations which are addressed to them, and are vain. The only wise man is he who says with the Apostle: I forbear, lest any man should think of me above that which he seeth me to be or that he heareth of me (2 Cor. xii. 6).

St. Bernard of
Clairvaux. *Letter VI.*

Additional Biblical Reflections: Psalm 119:33-35; Proverbs 1:7; Hosea 4:6-7.

Prayer

Dearest Lord, you are the way, the truth, and the life. Grant that we who pursue your way would seek both knowledge and delight of your truth so that we might truly experience the life that you have given us on account of your Son. In Jesus's name. Amen.

DAY 7

S t. Bernard tells us today that the genuine love of God is manifest when we feel pangs of the heart to the extent that we cannot love God more than we are capable of. These pangs come from our recognition and gratitude for God's love for us. That we cannot love God more than we are capable, as human beings, is a source of a holy lament not because we are insufficient—God made us as we are and declared us good—but because God's love is so magnificent.

Meditations from St. Bernard

The faithful know how much need they have of Jesus and Him crucified; but though they wonder and rejoice at the ineffable love made manifest in Him, they are not daunted at having no more than their own poor souls to give in return for such great and condescending charity. They love all the more, because they know themselves to be loved so exceedingly; but to whom little is given the same loveth little (Luke 7.47). Neither Jew nor pagan feels the pangs of love as doth the Church, which saith, 'Stay me with flagons, comfort me with apples; for I am sick of love' (Cant. 2.5). She beholds King Solomon, with the crown wherewith his mother crowned him in the day of his espousals; she sees the Sole-begotten of the Father bearing the heavy burden of His Cross; she sees the Lord of all power and might bruised and spat upon, the Author of life and glory transfixed with nails, smitten by the lance, overwhelmed with mockery, and at last laying

14

down His precious life for His friends. Contemplating this the sword of love pierces through her own soul also and she cried aloud, 'Stay me with flagons, comfort me with apples; for I am sick of love.' The fruits which the Spouse gathers from the Tree of Life in the midst of the garden of her Beloved, are pomegranates (Cant. 4.13), borrowing their taste from the Bread of heaven, and their color from the Blood of Christ. She sees death dying and its author overthrown: she beholds captivity led captive from hell to earth, from earth to heaven, so 'that at the name of Jesus every knee should bow, of things in heaven and things in earth and things under the earth' (Phil. 2.10). The earth under the ancient curse brought forth thorns and thistles; but now the Church beholds it laughing with flowers and restored by the grace of a new benediction. Mindful of the verse, 'My heart danceth for joy, and in my song will I praise Him', she refreshes herself with the fruits of His Passion which she gathers from the Tree of the Cross, and with the flowers of His Resurrection whose fragrance invites the frequent visits of her Spouse.

Then it is that He exclaims, 'Behold thou art fair, My beloved, yea pleasant: also our bed is green' (Cant. 1.16). She shows her desire for His coming and whence she hopes to obtain it; not because of her own merits but because of the flowers of that field which God hath blessed. Christ who willed to be conceived and brought up in Nazareth, that is, the town of branches, delights in such blossoms. Pleased by such heavenly fragrance the bridegroom rejoices to revisit the heart's chamber when He finds it adorned with fruits and decked with flowers—that is, meditating on the mystery of His Passion or on the glory of His Resurrection.

St. Bernard of
Clairvaux. *On Loving
God*, Ch. 3.

Additional Biblical Reflections: Deuteronomy 6:5; Luke 10:27; 1 John 5:3.

Prayer

Lord, you made our hearts and all our bodies. When our hearts ache for you more than we are capable of, it is a pious sentiment that stems from the very design with which you made us. Grant us a holy longing to love you even more than we are capable of, and let us rest in the merits of Christ, whose limitless love of us and love of you is ours on account of your gracious favor. Amen.

DAY 8

The glory of God is known through both His death and resurrection—His and ours! In today's meditation, we hear how, while our flesh remains corrupt, corruption dies in the crucifixion. In the resurrection, we are granted a new body, new flesh, without corruption so that we might love God in ways we cannot yet fathom.

Meditations from St. Bernard

The tokens of the Passion we recognize as the fruitage of the ages of the past, appearing in the fullness of time during the reign of sin and death (Gal. 4.4). But it is the glory of the Resurrection, in the new springtime of regenerating grace, that the fresh flowers of the later age come forth, whose fruit shall be given without measure at the general resurrection, when time shall be no more. And so it is written, 'The winter is past, the rain is over and gone, the flowers appear on the earth' (Cant. 2.11 f); signifying that summer has come back with Him who dissolves icy death into the spring of a new life and says, 'Behold, I make all things new' (Rev. 21.5). His Body sown in the grave has blossomed in the Resurrection (I Cor. 15.42); and in like manner our valleys and fields which were barren or frozen, as if dead, glow with reviving life and warmth.

The Father of Christ who makes all things new, is well pleased with the freshness of those flowers and fruits, and the beauty of the field which breathes forth such heavenly fragrance; and He says in benediction, 'See, the smell of My Son is as the smell of a field which the Lord hath blessed' (Gen. 27.27). Blessed to overflowing, indeed, since of His fullness have all we received (John 1.16). But the Bride may come when she pleases and gather flowers and fruits therewith to adorn the inmost recesses of her conscience; that the Bridegroom when He cometh may find the chamber of her heart redolent with perfume.

So it behoves us, if we would have Christ for a frequent guest, to fill our hearts with faithful meditations on the mercy He showed in dying for us, and on His mighty power in rising again from the dead. To this David testified when he sang, 'God spake once, and twice I have also heard the same; that power belongeth unto God; and that Thou, Lord, art merciful (Ps. 62.11f). And surely there is proof enough and to spare in that Christ died for our sins and rose again for our justification, and ascended into heaven that He might protect us from on high, and sent the Holy Spirit for our comfort. Hereafter He will come again for the consummation of our bliss. In His Death He displayed His mercy, in His Resurrection His power; both combine to manifest His glory.

St. Bernard of
Clairvaux. *On Loving
God,* Ch. 3.

Additional Biblical Reflections: Isaiah 26:19; 1 Corinthians 6:14; John 11:25.

Prayer

Lord, your love for us is manifest in both your death and resurrection. Let us embrace, likewise, our death and resurrection, so our death might not be a cause to lament, and our resurrection might grant us hope in your image. Together, may the cross and resurrection pattern revive our hearts so that we might love you and love one another as you first loved us. Amen.

DAY 9

In today's meditation, St. Bernard expounds on the many ways that the Lord has demonstrated His love for us—ways that we cannot possibly reciprocate. Yet, by simply recognizing this fact, we are driven to a holy posture of gratitude, which is pious, noble, and good.

Meditations from St. Bernard

What shall I render unto the Lord for all His benefits towards me?' (Ps. 116.12). Reason and natural justice alike move me to give up myself wholly to loving Him to whom I owe all that I have and am. But faith shows me that I should love Him far more than I love myself, as I come to realize that He hath given me not my own life only, but even Himself. Yet, before the time of full revelation had come, before the Word was made flesh, died on the Cross, came forth from the grave, and returned to His Father; before God had shown us how much He loved us by all this plenitude of grace, the commandment had been uttered, 'Thou shalt love the Lord thy God with all thine heart, and with all thy soul and with all thy might' (Deut. 6.5), that is, with all thy being, all thy knowledge, all thy powers. And it was not unjust for God to claim this from His own work and gifts. Why should not the creature love his Creator, who gave him the power to love? Why should he not love Him with all his being, since it is by His gift alone that he can do anything that is good? It was God's creative grace that out of nothingness raised us to the dignity of manhood; and from this appears our duty to love Him, and the justice of His claim to that love. But how infinitely is the benefit increased when we bethink ourselves of His fulfillment of the promise, 'thou, Lord, shalt save both man and beast: how excellent is Thy mercy, O Lord!' (Ps. 36.6f.). For we, who 'turned our glory into the similitude of a calf that eateth hay' (Ps. 106.20), by our evil deeds debased ourselves so that we might be compared unto the beasts that perish. I owe all that I am to Him who made me: but how can I pay my debt to Him who redeemed me, and in such wondrous wise? Creation was not so vast a work as redemption; for it is written of man and of all things that were made, 'He spake the word, and they were made' (Ps. 148.5). But to redeem that creation which sprang into being at His word, how much He spake, what wonders He wrought, what hardships He endured, what shames He suffered! Therefore what reward shall I give unto the Lord for all the benefits which He hath done unto me? In the first creation He gave me myself; but in His new creation He gave me Himself, and by that gift restored to me the self that I had lost. Created first and then restored, I owe Him myself twice over in return for myself. But what have I to offer Him for the gift of Himself? Could I multiply myself a thousand-fold and then give Him all, what would that be in comparison with God?

St. Bernard of
Clairvaux. *On Loving
God*, Ch. 5.

Additional Biblical Reflections: Psalm 51:17; Psalm 116:12; Hebrews 10:1–39.

Prayer

Lord, what could we possibly give to you that compares to what you have given us? Still, like the widow, who gave a greater portion of herself than the rich man, who gave greater quantities but less by comparison of his heart, you graciously accept our lives as living sacrifices—offerings greater than that of calves and bulls. Let us live gratefully and be so moved to dedicate our lives to you, the giver of life itself. Amen.

DAY 10

In today's meditation, we take a break from considering the primary topic in St. Bernard's writings and consider, rather, how we might better follow God by looking to the pious lives of the saints as an example. When we struggle to know how to love God, though our heart longs to love Him more, we can do no better than consider the examples of saints who loved God before us.

Meditations from St. Bernard

It is indeed always worth while to portray the illustrious lives of the saints, that they may serve as a mirror and an example, and give, as it were, a relish to the life of men on earth. For by this means in some sort they live among us, even after death, and many of those who are dead while they live are challenged and recalled by them to true life. But now especially is there need for it because holiness is rare, and it is plain that our age is lacking in men. So greatly, in truth, do we perceive that lack to have increased in our day that none can doubt that we are smitten by that saying, Because iniquity shall abound the love of many shall wax cold; and, as I suppose, he has come or is at hand of whom it is written, Want shall go before his face. If I mistake not, Antichrist is he whom famine and sterility of all good both precedes and accompanies. Whether therefore it is the herald of one now present or the harbinger of one who shall come immediately, the want is evident. I speak not of the crowd, I speak not of the vile multitude of the children of this world: I would have you lift up your eyes upon the very pillars of the Church.

St. Bernard of
Clairvaux, *Life of St.
Malachy of Armagh,*
Preface.

Additional Biblical Reflections: 1 Corinthians 11:1-34; 1 Thessalonians 1:6; Revelation 20:11-15.

Prayer

Lord, you have worked marvels in the hearts of your saints who, though born of earthly mothers, as we have been, became pious exemplars of the faith. Lift up such examples so that, like patterns, we might follow their examples, which were, in turn, patterned after the example of Christ. Amen.

DAY 11

When we suffer hardship, trials, or persecutions, we can know that Christ has already done the same. If we suffer, as He did, we no longer have a God who is absent in suffering but enters it alongside us, and, more than that, redeems suffering itself for our good. Today's meditation allows us to reflect on the solidarity we have with our Lord when we suffer.

Meditations from St. Bernard

How much I sympathize with your trouble only He knows who bore the griefs of all in His own body. How willingly would I advise you if I knew what to say, or help you if I were able, as efficaciously as I would wish that He who knows and can do all things should advise and assist me in all my necessities. If brother Drogo had consulted me about leaving your house I should by no means have agreed with him; and now that he has left, if he were to apply to enter into mine I should not receive him. All that I was able to do in those circumstances I have done for you, and have written, as you know, to the abbot who has received him. After this, reverend father, what is there more that I am able to do on your behalf? And as regards yourself, your Holiness knows well with me that men are accustomed to be perfected not only in hope, but also to glory in tribulation. The Scripture consoles them, saying: The furnace proveth the potter's vessels, and temptation the righteous man (Ecclus. xxvii. 6, Vulg.); *The Lord is nigh unto them that are of a contrite heart (Ps. xxxiv. 18); and We must through much tribulation enter into the kingdom of God (Acts xiv. 21); and All who will live godly in Christ suffer persecution (2 Tim. iii. 12). Yet none the less ought we to sympathize with our friends whom we see placed in care and grief; because we do not know what will be the issue of such, and fear lest it may be for ill; since whilst, indeed, to saints and the elect tribulation worketh patience, patience experience, experience hope, and hope maketh not ashamed (Rom. v. 3–5), to the condemnable and reprobate, on the contrary, tribulation causes discouragement, and discouragement confusion, and confusion despair, which destroys them.*

In order, then, that this dreadful tempest may not submerge you, nor the frightful abyss swallow you up, and the unfathomable pit shut her mouth upon you, employ all the efforts of your prudence not to be overcome of evil, but to overcome evil with good. You will overcome if you fix solidly your hope in God, and wait patiently the issue of the affair. If that monk shall return to a sense of his duty, whether for fear of you, or because of his own painful condition, well and good; but if not, it is good for you to humble yourself under the mighty hand of God, nor to wish uselessly to resist His supreme ordering; because if it is of God it cannot be undone?

St. Bernard of
Clairvaux, *Letter to the
Abbot of Satin Nicasius
at Rheims.*

Additional Biblical Reflections: Philippians 3:10; James 1:2-4; 1 Peter 5:10.

Prayer

Lord, you are the great redeemer. Even the curse we earned for our sin—the curse of death and suffering—has been redeemed in your Son. May your cross be ever before our eyes during our trials and tribulations so that we might see that, in you, the path of suffering is one that leads to glory in your resurrection. Amen.

DAY 12

There is no mathematical equation that can "balance" out the debt of love we owe God. Rather, St. Bernard suggests that we love God immeasurably as He loves us immeasurably. Our limits to love are set only by our capacity. However, in Him, we also have an eternal existence whereby we might love God each day with all that we are.

Meditations from St. Bernard

Admit that God deserves to be loved very much, yea, boundlessly, because He loved us first, He infinite and we nothing, loved us, miserable sinners, with a love so great and so free. This is why I said at the beginning that the measure of our love to God is to love immeasurably. For since our love is toward God, who is infinite and immeasurable, how can we bound or limit the love we owe Him? Besides, our love is not a gift but a debt. And since it is the Godhead who loves us, Himself boundless, eternal, supreme love, of whose greatness there is no end, yea, and His wisdom is infinite, whose peace passeth all understanding; since it is He who loves us, I say, can we think of repaying Him grudgingly? 'I will love Thee, O Lord, my strength. The Lord is my rock and my fortress and my deliverer, my God, my strength, in whom I will trust' (Ps. 18.1f). He is all that I need, all that I long for. My God and my help, I will love Thee for Thy great goodness; not so much as I might, surely, but as much as I can. I cannot love Thee as Thou deservest to be loved, for I cannot love Thee more than my own feebleness permits. I will love Thee more when Thou deemest me worthy to receive greater capacity for loving; yet never so perfectly as Thou hast deserved of me. 'Thine eyes did see my substance, yet being unperfect; and in Thy book all my members were written' (PS. 139.16). Yet Thou recordest in that book all who do what they can, even though they cannot do what they ought. Surely I have said enough to show how God should be loved and why. But who has felt, who can know, who express, how much we should love him.

St. Bernard of
Clairvaux. *On Loving
God*, Ch. 6.

Additional Biblical Reflections: Romans 8:28-29; Ephesians 2:4-5; 1 John 4:7-16.

Prayer

Lord, your love is great and eternal. While we cannot match you in the measure of our love, you have granted us a share in eternity. Therefore, our love for you may also be immeasurable as we enjoy eternal life in you. Grant us the ability to love you immeasurably every day of our eternal lives. Amen.

DAY 13

L oving God cannot be a contractual agreement whereby we receive certain benefits in exchange for our love. The love of God does not merit God's benefits, but it does receive them—not for the sake of earning spiritual profits, but as spontaneous as love is itself. For, loving God is its own reward.

Meditations from St. Bernard

And now let us consider what profit we shall have from loving God. Even though our knowledge of this is imperfect, still that is better than to ignore it altogether. I have already said (when it was a question of wherefore and in what manner God should be loved) that there was a double reason constraining us: His right and our advantage. Having written as best I can, though unworthily, of God's right to be loved. I have still to treat of the recompense which that love brings. For although God would be loved without respect of reward, yet He wills not to leave love unrewarded. True charity cannot be left destitute, even though she is unselfish and seeketh not her own (I Cor. 13.5). Love is an affection of the soul, not a contract: it cannot rise from a mere agreement, nor is it so to be gained. It is spontaneous in its origin and impulse; and true love is its own satisfaction. It has its reward; but that reward is the object beloved. For whatever you seem to love, if it is on account of something else, what you do really love is that something else, not the apparent object of desire. St. Paul did not preach the

28

Gospel that he might earn his bread; he ate that he might be strengthened for his ministry. What he loved was not bread, but the Gospel. True love does not demand a reward, but it deserves one. Surely no one offers to pay for love; yet some recompense is due to one who loves, and if his love endures he will doubtless receive it.

St. Bernard of
Clairvaux. *On Loving
God*, Ch. 7.

Additional Biblical Reflections: Deuteronomy 7:9; 1 Corinthians 12:1-13; Colossians 3:14.

Prayer

Lord, loving you is its own reward. Let us not love you as we consume goods or services, expecting certain payments for our hearts' investments. Rather, let us love recklessly, spontaneously, without reason or rationality, and simply receive whatever benefits such love might bring upon us on account of your graciousness. Amen.

DAY 14

Once again, in today's meditation, St. Bernard bids us to consider the significance of persecutions and sufferings we must endure as the Faithful. Here, St. Bernard offers several Biblical examples of how those who have been persecuted endured and were blessed on account of their sufferings.

Meditations from St. Bernard

I have learned with much pain by your letter the persecution that you are enduring for the sake of righteousness, and although the consolation given you by Christ in the promise of His kingdom may suffice amply for you, none the less is it my duty to render you both all the consolation that is in my power, and sound and faithful advice as far as I am able. For who can see without anxiety Peter stretching his arms in the midst of the billows?— or hear without grief the dove of Christ not singing, but groaning as if she said, How shall we sing the Lord's song in a strange land? (Ps. cxxxvii. 4). Who, I say, can without tears look upon the tears of Christ Himself, who from the bottom of the abyss lifts now His eyes unto the hills to see from whence cometh His help? But we to whom in your humility you say that you are looking, are not mountains of help, but are ourselves struggling with laborious endeavours in this vale of tears against the snares of a resisting enemy, and the violence of worldly malice, and with you we cry out, Our help is from the Lord, who made Heaven and earth (Ps. cxxi. 2).

All those, indeed, who wish to live piously in Christ suffer persecution (2 Tim. iii. 12). The intention to live piously is never wanting to them, but it is not always possible to carry it perfectly out, for just as it is the mark of the wicked constantly to struggle against the pious designs of the good; so it is not a reproach to the piety [of the latter], even although they are frequently unable to perfect their just and holy desires, because they are few against many opposers. Thus Aaron yielded against his will to the impious clamours of the riotous people (Exod. xxxii.). So Samuel unwillingly anointed Saul, constrained by the too eager desires of the same people for a king (1 Sam. x.). So David, when he wished to build a Temple, yet because of the numerous wars which that valorous man had constantly to sustain against enemies who molested him, he was forbidden to do what he piously proposed (2 Sam. vii.). Similarly, venerable father, I counsel you, without prejudice to the better advice of wiser persons, so to soften, for the present only, the rigour of your purpose of reform, and that of those who share it with you, that you may not be unmindful of the salvation of the weaker brethren. Those, indeed, over whom you have consented to preside in that Order of Cluny ought to be invited to a stricter life, but they ought not to be obliged to embrace it against their will. I believe that those who do desire to live more strictly ought to be persuaded either to bear with the weaker out of charity as far as they can without sin, or permitted to preserve the customs which they desire in the monastery itself, if that may be done without scandal to either party; or at least that they should be set free from the Order to associate themselves where it may seem good with other brothers who live according to their proposal.

St. Bernard of
Clairvaux. *To Simon,
Abbot of S. Nicholas.*

Additional Biblical Reflections: Jeremiah 20:11; Luke 6:22; 2 Timothy 3:12.

Prayer

Lord, the examples of the many persecuted saints whom you have preserved are many. Grant that should we face persecution in this life, we might likewise be granted a steadfast and holy endurance to see through our sufferings to the glories of eternity with you. Amen.

DAY 15

S t. Bernard calls love one of humanity's "natural" affections. God made us that way. We love, but the object of our love is, at least in our carnal condition, more often the self than others. We tend to love God insofar as He satisfies our self-love—so long as He meets our needs and expectations. Thus, our love must be perfected in the image of the Son. Our self-will must die with Christ that we might be raised with godly desires.

Meditations from St. Bernard

Love is one of the four natural affections, which it is needless to name since everyone knows them. And because love is natural, it is only right to love the Author of nature first of all. Hence comes the first and great commandment, 'Thou shalt love the Lord thy God.' But nature is so frail and weak that necessity compels her to love herself first; and this is carnal love, wherewith man loves himself first and selfishly, as it is written, 'That was not first which is spiritual but that which is natural; and afterward that which is spiritual' (I Cor. 15.46). This is not as the precept ordains but as nature directs: 'No man ever yet hated his own flesh' (Eph. 5.29). But if, as is likely, this same love should grow excessive and, refusing to be contained within the restraining banks of necessity, should overflow into the fields of voluptuousness, then a command checks the flood, as if by a dike: 'Thou shalt love thy neighbor as thyself'. And this is right: for he who shares our nature should share our love, itself the fruit of nature. Wherefore if a man find it a burden, I will not say only to relieve his brother's needs, but to minister to his brother's pleasures, let him mortify those same affections in himself, lest he become a transgressor. He may cherish himself as tenderly as he chooses, if only he remembers to show the same indulgence to his neighbor. This is the curb of temperance imposed on thee, O man, by the law of life and conscience, lest thou shouldest follow thine own lusts to destruction, or become enslaved by those passions which are the enemies of thy true welfare. Far better divide thine enjoyments with thy neighbor than with these enemies. And if, after the counsel of the son of Sirach, thou goest not after thy desires but refrainest thyself from thine appetites (Ecclus. 18.30); if according to the apostolic precept having food and raiment thou art therewith content (I Tim. 6.8), then thou wilt find it easy to abstain from fleshly lusts which war against the soul, and to divide with thy neighbors what thou hast refused to thine own desires. That is a temperate and righteous love which practices self-denial in order to minister to a brother's necessity. So our selfish love grows truly social, when it includes our neighbors in its circle... But if we are to love our neighbors as we ought, we must have regard to God also: for it is only in God that we can pay that debt of love aright. Now a man cannot love his neighbor in God, except he love God Himself; wherefore we must love God first, in order to love our neighbors in Him. This too, like all good things, is the Lord's doing, that we should love Him, for He hath endowed us with the possibility of love. He who created nature sustains it; nature is so constituted that its Maker is its protector for ever. Without Him nature could not have begun to be; without Him it could not subsist at all. That we might not be ignorant of this, or vainly attribute to ourselves the beneficence of our Creator, God has determined in the depths of His wise counsel that we should be subject to tribulations. So when man's strength fails and God comes to his aid, it is meet and right that man, rescued by God's hand, should glorify Him, as it is written, 'Call upon Me in the time of trouble; so will I hear thee, and thou shalt praise Me' (Ps. 50.15). In such wise man, animal and carnal by nature, and loving only himself, begins to love God by reason of that very self-love; since he learns that in God he can accomplish all things that are good, and that without God he can do nothing.

St. Bernard of
Clairvaux. *On Loving
God*, Ch. 8.

Additional Biblical Reflections: Matthew 26:41; Romans 8:8-13; Galatians 5:19-21.

Prayer

Lord, refine our nature. Use the capacity we have to love and direct it toward you and others. In doing so, make us more closely resemble your Son, who loved us perfectly without any thought of self. Amen.

DAY 16

Love begins selfishly. However, this is but one step toward refining our love for what St. Bernard calls the second and third degrees of love—ultimately ending up loving God on His own account solely because He is God. Thus, let us examine our self-love and, from there, learn how to progress in our love rather than continue to turn it inward toward one's own interests, passions, and desires.

Meditations from St. Bernard

So then in the beginning man loves God, not for God's sake, but for his own. It is something for him to know how little he can do by himself and how much by God's help, and in that knowledge to order himself rightly towards God, his sure support. But when tribulations, recurring again and again, constrain him to turn to God for unfailing help, would not even a heart as hard as iron, as cold as marble, be softened by the goodness of such a Savior, so that he would love God not altogether selfishly, but because He is God? Let frequent troubles drive us to frequent supplications; and surely, tasting, we must see how gracious the Lord is (Ps. 34.8). Thereupon His goodness once realized draws us to love Him unselfishly, yet more than our own needs impel us to love Him selfishly: even as the Samaritans told the woman who announced that it was Christ who was at the well: 'Now we believe, not because of thy saying: for we have heard Him ourselves, and know that this is indeed the Christ, the savior of the world' (John 4.42). We likewise bear the same witness to our own fleshly nature, saying, 'No longer do we love God because of our necessity, but because we have tasted and seen how gracious the Lord is'. Our temporal wants have a speech of their own, proclaiming the benefits they have received from God's favor. Once this is recognized it will not be hard to fulfill the commandment touching love to our neighbors; for whosoever loves God aright loves all God's creatures. Such love is pure, and finds no burden in the precept bidding us purify our souls, in obeying the truth through the Spirit unto unfeigned love of the brethren (I Peter 1.22). Loving as he ought, he counts that command only just. Such love is thankworthy, since it is spontaneous; pure, since it is shown not in word nor tongue, but in deed and truth (I John 3.18); just, since it repays what it has received. Whoso loves in this fashion, loves even as he is loved, and seeks no more his own but the things which are Christ's, even as Jesus sought not His own welfare, but ours, or rather ourselves. Such was the psalmist's love when he sang: 'O give thanks unto the Lord, for He is gracious' (Ps. 118.1). Whosoever praises God for His essential goodness, and not merely because of the benefits He has bestowed, does really love God for God's sake, and not selfishly. The psalmist was not speaking of such love when he said: 'So long as thou doest well unto thyself, men will speak good of thee'(Ps. 49.18). The third degree of love, we have now seen, is to love God on His own account, solely because He is God.

St. Bernard of
Clairvaux. *On Loving
God*, Ch. 9

Additional Biblical Reflections: Psalm 49; John 4:42; 1 Peter 1:22.

Prayer

Lord, while we begin to learn to love through the love of self, let us love ourselves not on account of ego but because you love us too. For, how can we not love ourselves if we hope to fashion our hearts after yours? Let this be a holy love, though, that persists not for our own sake but for the sake of your Son. Amen.

DAY 17

Yesterday's prayer led us toward what St. Bernard calls the fourth degree of love—"wherein one loves himself only in God." While we might be tempted to believe that the cure of self-love is self-hatred, to hate oneself is to hate one whom God Himself loves! The command to love one's neighbor as oneself cannot be fulfilled without loving ourselves properly. For if we hated ourselves, to love one's neighbor as we do ourselves would not be to love him or her at all. If we desire to have hearts that reflect God's, we must learn to love ourselves like God does.

Meditations from St. Bernard

How blessed is he who reaches the fourth degree of love, wherein one loves himself only in God! Thy righteousness standeth like the strong mountains, O God. Such love as this is God's hill, in the which it pleaseth Him to dwell. 'Who shall ascend into the hill of the Lord?' 'O that I had wings like a dove; for then would I flee away and be at rest.' 'At Salem is His tabernacle; and His dwelling in Sion.' 'Woe is me, that I am constrained to dwell with Mesech!' (Ps. 24.3; 55.6; 76.2; 120.5). When shall this flesh and blood, this earthen vessel which is my soul's tabernacle, attain thereto? When shall my soul, rapt with divine love and altogether self-forgetting, yea, become like a broken vessel, yearn wholly for God, and, joined unto the Lord, be one spirit with Him?

When shall she exclaim, 'My flesh and my heart faileth; but God is the strength of my heart and my portion for ever' (Ps. 73.26). I would count him blessed and holy to whom such rapture has been vouchsafed in this mortal life, for even an instant to lose thyself, as if thou wert emptied and lost and swallowed up in God, is no human love; it is celestial. But if sometimes a poor mortal feels that heavenly joy for a rapturous moment, then this wretched life envies his happiness, the malice of daily trifles disturbs him, this body of death weighs him down, the needs of the flesh are imperative, the weakness of corruption fails him, and above all brotherly love calls him back to duty. Alas! that voice summons him to re-enter his own round of existence; and he must ever cry out lamentably, 'O Lord, I am oppressed: undertake for me' (Isa. 38.14); and again, 'O wretched man that I am! who shall deliver me from the body of this death?' (Rom. 7.24).

In this life, I think, we cannot fully and perfectly obey that precept, 'Thou shalt love the Lord thy God with all thy heart, and with all thy soul, and with all thy strength, and with all thy mind' (Luke 10.27). For here the heart must take thought for the body; and the soul must energize the flesh; and the strength must guard itself from impairment. And by God's favor, must seek to increase. It is therefore impossible to offer up all our being to God, to yearn altogether for His face, so long as we must accommodate our purposes and aspirations to these fragile, sickly bodies of ours. Wherefore the soul may hope to possess the fourth degree of love, or rather to be possessed by it, only when it has been clothed upon with that spiritual and immortal body, which will be perfect, peaceful, lovely, and in everything wholly subjected to the spirit. And to this degree no human effort can attain: it is in God's power to give it to whom He wills. Then the soul will easily reach that highest stage, because no lusts of the flesh will retard its eager entrance into the joy of its Lord, and no troubles will disturb its peace. May we not think that the holy martyrs enjoyed this grace, in some degree at least, before they laid down their victorious bodies? Surely that was immeasurable strength of love which enraptured their souls, enabling them to laugh at fleshly torments and to yield their lives gladly. But even though the frightful pain could not destroy their peace of mind, it must have impaired somewhat its perfection.

St. Bernard of
Clairvaux. *On Loving
God,* Ch. 10.

Additional Biblical Reflections: Leviticus 19:18; Matthew 22:1-46; Luke 10:27.

Prayer

Lord, you loved us when we were yet unlovable. Help us to love ourselves only through the lens of your longing gaze, which drove you not to puff us up in the ways of the flesh but love us to the point of sacrifice and death. Therefore, let us love ourselves in such a way that we are willing to crucify the flesh and see ourselves raised anew in our love of you. Amen.

DAY 18

To be apart from the body is to be with the Lord. However, as St. Bernard reminds us, our hope is not for a bodiless existence as souls floating around in God's heavenly glory. Rather, as we confess in the Creed, the resurrection of the body remains our hope. This impacts how we view our flesh—not as though it is the enemy of the soul, but as a part of the self that must be redeemed.

Meditations from St. Bernard

What of the souls already released from their bodies? We believe that they are overwhelmed in that vast sea of eternal light and of luminous eternity. But no one denies that they still hope and desire to receive their bodies again: whence it is plain that they are not yet wholly transformed, and that something of self remains yet unsurrendered. Not until death is swallowed up in victory, and perennial light overflows the uttermost bounds of darkness, not until celestial glory clothes our bodies, can our souls be freed entirely from self and give themselves up to God. For until then souls are bound to bodies, if not by a vital connection of sense, still by natural affection; so that without their bodies they cannot attain to their perfect consummation, nor would they if they could. And although there is no defect in the soul itself before the restoration of its body, since it has already attained to the highest state of which it is by itself capable, yet the spirit would not yearn for reunion with the flesh if without the flesh it could be consummated.

And finally, 'Right dear in the sight of the Lord is the death of His saints' (Ps. 116.15). But if their death is precious, what must such a life as theirs be! No wonder that the body shall seem to add fresh glory to the spirit; for though it is weak and mortal, it has availed not a little for mutual help. How truly he spake who said, 'All things work together for good to them that love God' (Rom. 8.28). The body is a help to the soul that loves God, even when it is ill, even when it is dead, and all the more when it is raised again from the dead: for illness is an aid to penitence; death is the gate of rest; and the resurrection will bring consummation. So, rightly, the soul would not be perfected without the body, since she recognizes that in every condition it has been needful to her good.

St. Bernard of
Clairvaux. *On Loving
God,* Ch. 11.

Additional Biblical Reflections: John 6:40; 2 Corinthians 4:14; Romans 6:5.

Prayer

Lord, you have made us in body and soul and declared our whole selves good. Let us not despise our bodies but despise only fleshly desire rooted in sin so that we might still hope for the redemption of our bodies along with our souls, as we await the new heaven and earth promised in your Word. Amen.

DAY 19

Many of us have laws unto ourselves that are not laws from the Lord. This may be beneficial or detrimental to our faith. Thus, we must make sure that any laws we establish for ourselves do not supplant God's law or revise how we apply God's truths to our lives. Therefore, the Scriptures declare that in the Spirit, the law ceases to be the burden so that to the flesh, it is but a delight.

Meditations from St. Bernard

Furthermore, the slave and the hireling have a law, not from the Lord, but of their own contriving; the one does not love God, the other loves something else more than God. They have a law of their own, not of God, I say; yet it is subject to the law of the Lord. For though they can make laws for themselves, they cannot supplant the changeless order of the eternal law. Each man is a law unto himself, when he sets up his will against the universal law, perversely striving to rival his Creator, to be wholly independent, making his will his only law. What a heavy and burdensome yoke upon all the sons of Adam, bowing down our necks, so that our life draweth nigh unto hell. 'O wretched man that I am! Who shall deliver me from the body of this death?' (Rom. 7.24). I am weighed down, I am almost overwhelmed, so that 'If the Lord had not helped me, it had not failed but my soul had been put to silence' (Ps. 94.17). Job was groaning under this load when he lamented: 'Why hast Thou set me as a mark against Thee,

43

so that I am a burden to myself?' (Job 7.20). He was a burden to himself through the law which was of his own devising: yet he could not escape God's law, for he was set as a mark against God. The eternal law of righteousness ordains that he who will not submit to God's sweet rule shall suffer the bitter tyranny of self: but he who wears the easy yoke and light burden of love (Matt. 11.30) will escape the intolerable weight of his own self-will. Wondrously and justly does that eternal law retain rebels in subjection, so that they are unable to escape. They are subject to God's power, yet deprived of happiness with Him, unable to dwell with God in light and rest and glory everlasting. O Lord my God, 'why dost Thou not pardon my transgression and take away mine iniquity?' (Job 7.21). Then freed from the weight of my own will, I can breathe easily under the light burden of love. I shall not be coerced by fear, nor allured by mercenary desires; for I shall be led by the Spirit of God, that free Spirit whereby Thy sons are led, which beareth witness with my spirit that I am among the children of God (Rom. 8.16). So shall I be under that law which is Thine; and as Thou art, so shall I be in the world. Whosoever do what the apostle bids, 'Owe no man anything, but to love one another' (Rom. 13.8), are doubtless even in this life conformed to God's likeness: they are neither slaves nor hirelings but sons.

St. Bernard of
Clairvaux. *On Loving
God*, Ch. 13.

Additional Biblical Reflections: Romans 8:15-23; Galatians 3:28; Ephesians 1:5.

Prayer

Lord, let us delight in your law so that we might better know your ways. For you have made us and know what is best for our lives. Grant this, so we might enjoy the gift of life and reflect your glory in all we say and do. Amen.

DAY 20

We live in a critical age—a time when many are willing to criticize others without understanding. Often, such attacks are waged out of the attacker's own flawed heart and insecurity. Thus, the Pharisees—insecure because the law they had followed offered no such security—attacked our Lord. Men of this stripe have existed in every generation, and such was the case in St. Bernard's day. In today's meditation, he offers encouragement to several abbots who have unfairly been assaulted in such a way.

Meditations from St. Bernard

Let those depart both from me and from You who say: We do not desire to he better than our fathers; declaring themselves to be the sons of lukewarm and lax persons, whose memory is in execration, since they have eaten sour grapes, and their children's teeth are set on edge. Or if they pretend that their fathers were holy men, whose memory is blessed, let them imitate their sanctity, and not defend, as laws instituted by them, the indulgences and dispensations which they have merely endured. Although holy Elias says, I am not better than my fathers (2 Kings xix. 4), yet he has not said that he did not wish to be. Jacob saw upon the ladder Angels ascending and descending (Gen. xxviii. 12); but was any one of them either sitting, or standing still? It was not for angels to stand still on the uncertain rounds of a frail ladder; nor can anything remain fixed in the same condition during the uncertain period of this mortal life. Here have we no continuing city; nor do we yet possess, but always seek for, that which is to come. Of necessity you either ascend or descend, and if you try to stand still you cannot but fall. It may be held as certain that the man is not good at all who does not wish to be better; and where you begin not to care to make advance in goodness there also you leave off being good.

Let those depart both from me and from you who call good evil and evil good. If they call the pursuit of righteousness evil, what good thing will be good in their eyes? The Lord once spoke a single word, and the Pharisees were scandalized (S. Matt. xv. 12). But now these new Pharisees are scandalized not even at a word, but at silence. You plainly see then that they seek only the occasion to attack you. But leave them alone; they be blind leaders of the blind. Take thought for the salvation of the little ones, not of the murmurs of the evil-disposed. Why do you so much fear to give scandal to those who are not to be cured unless you become sick with them? It is not even desirable to wait to see whether your resolutions are pleasing to all of you in all respects, otherwise you will determine upon little or no good. You ought to consult not the views, but the needs of all; and faithfully to draw them towards God, even although they be unwilling, rather than abandon them to the desires of their heart. I commend myself to your holy prayers.

St. Bernard of
Clairvaux, *To the Abbots
Assembled at Soissons.*

Additional Biblical Reflections: Matthew 15:12; Romans 12:2; Philippians 3:23.

Prayer

Lord, we are easily swayed by our times. Let us not be taken captive by hollow philosophies but may our consciences be bound to your truth. Let us, nonetheless, learn to love in the way of your Incarnation in the world, as we find it not as we would have it be. In Jesus's name. Amen.

DAY 21

The law of God alone evokes reason to fear. For, when we measure ourselves up to the standard of the law, we fall short. However, when accompanying the law, love rescues us of such fear. It turns the fulfillment of love into a godly fear—a reverence for the mysteries of God—and even joy.

Meditations from St. Bernard

Now the children have their law, even though it is written, 'The law is not made for a righteous man' (I Tim. 1.9). For it must be remembered that there is one law having to do with the spirit of servitude, given to fear, and another with the spirit of liberty, given in tenderness. The children are not constrained by the first, yet they could not exist without the second: even as St. Paul writes, 'Ye have not received the spirit of bondage again to fear; but ye have received the spirit of adoption, whereby we cry, Abba, Father' (Rom. 8.15). And again to show that that same righteous man was not under the law, he says: 'To them that are under the law, I became as under the law, that I might gain them that are under the law; to them that are without law, as without law (being not without law to God, but under the law to Christ)' (I Cor. 9.20f). So it is rightly said, not that the righteous do not have a law, but, 'The law is not made for a righteous man', that is, it is not imposed on rebels but freely given to those willingly obedient, by Him whose goodness established it. Wherefore the Lord saith meekly: 'Take My yoke upon you', which may be paraphrased thus: 'I do not force it on you, if you are reluctant; but if you will you may bear it. Otherwise it will be weariness, not rest, that you shall find for your souls.'

Love is a good and pleasant law; it is not only easy to bear, but it makes the laws of slaves and hirelings tolerable; not destroying but completing them; as the Lord saith: 'I am not come to destroy the law, but to fulfill' (Matt. 5.17). It tempers the fear of the slave, it regulates the desires of the hireling, it mitigates the severity of each. Love is never without fear, but it is godly fear. Love is never without desire, but it is lawful desire. So love perfects the law of service by infusing devotion; it perfects the law of wages by restraining covetousness. Devotion mixed with fear does not destroy it, but purges it.

St. Bernard of
Clairvaux. *On Loving
God*, Ch. 14

Additional Biblical Reflections: Joshua 1:9; Isaiah 41:10; 1 John 4:18.

Prayer

Lord, perfect your love within us so that all fear might be cast out and replaced with godly reverence. For, you do not desire that we would be timid creatures consumed by terror but confident children of you, our Father, who revere your law and live according to your will. Amen.

DAY 22

The flesh, St. Bernard says, is where we begin but not where we should end. From the beginnings in the flesh, by God's grace, we must proceed through degrees so that in the spirit we come to know more than what we see merely by the flesh. In this way, we come to know true love and thereby enter God's joy and the plenteousness of His house.

Meditations from St. Bernard

Nevertheless, since we are carnal and are born of the lust of the flesh, it must be that our desire and our love shall have its beginning in the flesh. But rightly guided by the grace of God through these degrees, it will have its consummation in the spirit: for that was not first which is spiritual but that which is natural; and afterward that which is spiritual (I Cor. 15.46). And we must bear the image of the earthy first, before we can bear the image of the heavenly. At first, man loves himself for his own sake. That is the flesh, which can appreciate nothing beyond itself. Next, he perceives that he cannot exist by himself, and so begins by faith to seek after God, and to love Him as something necessary to his own welfare. That is the second degree, to love God, not for God's sake, but selfishly. But when he has learned to worship God and to seek Him aright, meditating on God, reading God's Word, praying and obeying His commandments, he comes gradually to know what God is, and finds Him altogether lovely. So, having tasted and seen how gracious the Lord is (Ps. 34.8), he advances to the third degree, when he loves God, not merely as his benefactor but as God. Surely he must remain long in this state; and I know not whether it would be possible to make further progress in this life to that fourth degree and perfect condition wherein man loves himself solely for God's sake. Let any who have attained so far bear record; I confess it seems beyond my powers. Doubtless it will be reached when the good and faithful servant shall have entered into the joy of his Lord (Matt. 25.21), and been satisfied with the plenteousness of God's house (Ps. 36.8). For then in wondrous wise he will forget himself and as if delivered from self, he will grow wholly God's. Joined unto the Lord, he will then be one spirit with Him (I Cor. 6.17). This was what the prophet meant, I think, when he said: ' I will go forth in the strength of the Lord God: and will make mention of Thy righteousness only' (Ps. 71.16). Surely he knew that when he should go forth in the spiritual strength of the Lord, he would have been freed from the infirmities of the flesh, and would have nothing carnal to think of, but would be wholly filled in his spirit with the righteousness of the Lord.

St. Bernard of
Clairvaux. *On Loving
God*, Ch. 15.

Additional Biblical Reflections: Proverbs 3:3-8; Psalm 101:1-8; 2 Corinthians 5:16-18.

Prayer

Lord, you have granted us lives in this world not that we might lament or feel pain alone but progress toward you in the way of the Spirit. Thus, you sent your Spirit into the world. We also pray that you would send your Spirit into our hearts and that our lives might follow an upward path toward your glory. Amen.

DAY 23

O ur lives are not lives of wandering. Rather, they are lives fixed on a destination. The destination has been determined by God and is revealed in the Word. Namely, it is life in the Kingdom of God. Today's meditation from St. Bernard helps us focus our eyes on our ultimate hope in His Kingdom.

Meditations from St. Bernard

In that day the members of Christ can say of themselves what St. Paul testified concerning their Head: 'Yea, though we have known Christ after the flesh, yet now henceforth know we Him no more' (II Cor. 5.16). None shall thereafter know himself after the flesh; for 'flesh and blood cannot inherit the Kingdom of God' (I Cor. 15.50). Not that there will be no true substance of the flesh, but all carnal needs will be taken away, and the love of the flesh will be swallowed up in the love of the spirit, so that our weak human affections will be made divinely strong. Then the net of charity which as it is drawn through the great and wide sea doth not cease to gather every kind of fish, will be drawn to the shore; and the bad will be cast away, while only the good will be kept (Matt. 13.48). In this life the net of all-including love gathers every kind of fish into its wide folds, becoming all things to all men, sharing adversity or prosperity, rejoicing with them that do rejoice, and weeping with them that weep (Rom. 12.15). But when the net is drawn to shore, whatever causes pain will be rejected, like the bad fish, while only what is pleasant and joyous will be kept. Do you not recall how St. Paul said: 'Who is weak and I am not weak? Who is offended and I burn not?' And yet weakness and offense were far from him. So too he bewailed many which had sinned already and had not repented, though he was neither the sinner nor the penitent. But there is a city made glad by the rivers of the flood of grace (Ps. 46.4), and whose gates the Lord loveth more than all the dwellings of Jacob (Ps. 87.2). In it is no place for lamentation over those condemned to everlasting fire, prepared for the devil and his angels (Matt. 25.41). In these earthly dwellings, though men may rejoice, yet they have still other battles to fight, other mortal perils to undergo. But in the heavenly Fatherland no sorrow nor sadness can enter: as it is written, 'The habitation of all rejoicing ones is in Thee' (Ps. 87. 7, Vulg.); and again, 'Everlasting joy shall be unto them' (Isa. 61.7). Nor could they recall things piteous, for then they will make mention of God's righteousness only. Accordingly, there will be no need for the exercise of compassion, for no misery will be there to inspire pity.

St. Bernard of
Clairvaux. *On Loving
God*, Ch. 15.

Additional Biblical Reflections: 1 Corinthians 9:24-25; Hebrews 10:26; Titus 3:5.

Prayer

Lord, let us live our lives with our eyes firmly fixed on the destination that is your Kingdom. Thus, we pray that thy Kingdom is not only realized in the world but likewise in our hearts and lives. Amen.

DAY 24

In today's meditation, St. Bernard writes to an abbot who, having written to Bernard for advice, had recently seen several monks—or "religious" persons—depart his monastery and is questioning whether it might be his fault. At first, Bernard struggles to offer a response, not knowing the full context or cause by which many left. However, regardless of the cause, he begs the abbot to consider the situation as a mirror—what might he learn from the occurrence? How might the Lord be using this situation to refine His service?

Meditations from St. Bernard

You write to me from beyond the sea to ask of me advice which I should have preferred that you had sought from some other. I am held between two difficulties, for if I do not reply to you, you may take my silence for a sign of contempt; but if I do reply I cannot avoid danger, since whatever I reply I must of necessity either give scandal to some one or give to some other a security which they ought not to have, or at all events more than they ought to have. That your brethren have departed from you was not with the knowledge nor by the advice or persuasion of me or of my brethren. But I incline to believe that it was of God, since their purpose could not be shaken by all your efforts; and that the brethren themselves thought this also who so earnestly sought my advice about themselves; their conscience troubling them, as I suppose, because they quitted you.

Here is a mirror. In it let your Religious consider, not the features of their faces, but the fact of their turning back. Here let them determine and distinguish their motives, their thoughts, accusing or excusing them with that sentence which the spiritual man passes who judges all things, and is himself judged by no one. I, indeed, cannot rashly determine whether the state which they have left or that which they have embraced was the greater or less, the higher or lower, the severer or the more lax. Let them judge according to the rule of S. Gregory. But to you, Reverend Father, I declare, with as much positive assurance as plain truth, that it is not at all desirable that you should set yourself to quench the Spirit. Hinder not him, it is said, who is able to do good, but if thou canst, do good also thyself (Prov. iii. 27, Vulg.). It more befits you to be proud of the good works of your sons, since a wise son is the glory of his father (Prov. x. 1). For the rest, let no one make it a cause of complaint against me that I have not hidden in my heart the righteousness of God, unless, perhaps, I have spoken less of it than I ought, for the sake of avoiding scandal.

St. Bernard of
Clairvaux, *To the Abbot
of a Certain Monastery at
York.*

Additional Biblical Reflections: Matthew 13:11; Ephesians 3:2-6; Colossians 2:1-3.

Prayer

Lord, you work in mysterious ways. Let us find solace not in our examination of the ways by which you appear to be acting but rather in our knowledge of you and your character. For, all who love you, you are constantly working all things for our good, even redeeming our flaws for your sake. In Jesus's name. Amen.

DAY 25

In today's meditation, St. Bernard praises an abbot not for his personal piety or religious action but on account of his charity and love of the poor. Here, we see that what merits more in God's sight is not our commitment to ritual or prayer, but when such things launch us toward lives steeped in love and charity.

Meditations from St. Bernard

To the very dear father and Reverend Lord Thurstan, by the Grace of God Archbishop of York, Bernard, Abbot of Clairvaux, wishes the fullest health.

The general good report of men, as I have experienced, has said nothing in your favour which the splendour of your good works does not justify. Your actions, in fact, show that your high reputation, which fame had previously spread everywhere, was neither false nor ill-founded, but manifest and certain. Especially of late how brilliantly has your zeal for righteousness and your sacerdotal energy shone forth in the defence of the poor Religious who had no other helper. Once, indeed, the whole assembly of the saints used to venerate your works of mercy and alms deeds; but in doing so it narrated always what is common to you with very many, since whosoever possesses the goods of this world is bound to share them with the poor. But this is your episcopal task, this the noble proof of your paternal affection, this your truly divine fervour, the zeal which no doubt has inspired and aroused in you who makes His angels spirits and His ministers a flaming fire. This, I say, belongs entirely to you. It is the ornament of your dignity, the badge of your office, the adornment of your crown. It is one thing to fill the belly of the hungry, and quite another thing to have a zeal for holy poverty. The one serves nature, the other grace. Thou shalt visit thy kind, He says, and thou shalt not sin (Job v. 24, Vulg.). Therefore he who nourishes the flesh of another sins not in so doing, but he who honours the sanctity of another does good to his own soul; therefore he says again, Keep your alms in your own hand until you shall find a righteous man to whom to give it. For what advantage? Because He who receives a righteous man in the name of a righteous man shall receive a righteous man's reward (S. Matt. x. 41). Let us, then, discharge the debt that nature requires of us, that we may avoid sin; but let us be co-workers with grace, that we may merit to become sharers of it. It is this that I so admire in you, as I acknowledge that it was given to you from above. O, Father, truly reverend and to be regarded with the sincerest affection; the praise for what you have laid out of your temporal means to the relief of our necessities, will be blended with the praises of God for ever.

St. Bernard of
Clairvaux, *To Thurstan,*
Archbishop of York.

Additional Biblical Reflections: Proverbs 19:17; Luke 12:22; 1 John 3:17.

Prayer

Lord, you have given us all things, even your Son, without cause or merit. Let us also be cheerful givers so that we might be your instruments of love for the sake of the poor and all those in need. Amen.

DAY 26

I n today's mediation, St. Bernard praises a monastic community for continuing to strive toward greater degrees of holiness despite how praiseworthy they already are.

Meditations from St. Bernard

How marvellous are those things which I have heard and learned, and which the two Geoffries have announced to me, that you have become newly fervent with the fire from on high, that from weakness you have become strong, that you have flourished again with new sanctity.

This is the finger of God secretly working, softly renewing, healthfully changing not, indeed, bad men into good, but making good men better. Who will grant unto me to cross over to you and see this great sight? For that progress in holiness is not less wonderful or less delightful than that conversion. It is much more easy, in fact, to find many men of the world converted to good than one Religious who is good becoming better than he is. The rarest bird in the world is the monk who ascends ever so little from the point which he has once reached in the religious life. Thus the spectacle which you present, dearest brethren, is the more rare and salutary, not only to men who desire greatly to be the helper of your sanctity, but it rightly rejoices the whole Church of God as well; since the rarer it is the more glorious it is also. For prudence made it a duty to you to pass beyond that mediocrity so dangerously near to defect, and to escape from that lukewarmness which provokes God to reject you, it was even a duty of conscience for you to do so, since you know that it is not safe for men who have embraced the holy Rule to halt before having attained the goal to which it leads. I am exceedingly grieved that I am obliged by the pressing obligations of the day and the haste of the messenger to express the fulness of my affection with a pen so briefs and to comprise the breadth of my kindness for you within the narrow limits of this billet. But if anything is wanting, brother Geoffrey will supply it by word of mouth.

St. Bernard of
Clairvaux, *To Richard,
Abbot of Fountains, And
His Companions.*

Additional Biblical Reflections: Matthew 5:48; James 1:4; 1 John 2:5.

Prayer

Lord, you are perfect, and no matter how far we progress in this life, we fall short of your glory. Therefore, let us never grow weary of spiritual progress so that we might come to know you and your glory all the more in your presence until all is finally revealed on the last day. Amen.

DAY 27

When Bernard was separated from his Monks at Clairvaux, he did not write them solely so that they might have their longing for his return pacified, but because he genuinely found that he was more enriched by his brothers than they were by him. We must never forget that God has called us into holy communities of faith so that, as members of His body, we might grow together in holiness.

Meditations from St. Bernard

To his dearly-loved brethren the Monks of Clairvaux, the converts, and the novices, their brother Bernard sends greeting, bidding them rejoice in the Lord always. Judge by yourselves what I am suffering. If my absence is painful to you, let no one doubt that it is far more painful to me. The loss is not equal, the burden is not the same, for you are deprived of but one individual, while I am bereft of all of you. It cannot but be that I am weighed down by as many anxieties as you are in number; I grieve for the absence of each one of you, and fear the dangers which may attack you. This double grief will not leave me until I am restored to my children.

And since you know these things, you must not be angry at my long absence, which is not according to my will, but is due to the necessities of the Church; rather pity me. I hope that it will not be a long absence now; do you pray that it may not be unfruitful. Let any losses which may in the meantime happen to befall you be regarded as gains, for the cause is God's. And since He is gracious and all-powerful, He will easily make any losses good, and even add greater riches. Therefore, let us be of good courage, since we have God with us, in whom I am present with you, though we may seem to be separated by a long distance.

St. Bernard of
Clairvaux, *To His Monks
of Clairvaux.*

Additional Biblical Reflections: Acts 2:43-47; Colossians 1:18; Hebrews 10:25.

Prayer

Lord, your Church is your Bride. Spare us of the notion that we might love you, the Bridegroom, while we reject your Bride. Grant us the holy consolation of our fellow believers so that we might recognize your presence in our lives through their holy company. Amen.

DAY 28

The unity of the Church is a mystery. However, when we live charitably together as believers and follow the Lord, we find that all the Church benefits. However, when dissension and pride threaten the body, we find that all of us fall far from God's presence. Today, St. Bernard reminds us of the importance of our unity as His believers.

Meditations from St. Bernard

Let no one among you who shows himself attentive to his duties, humble, reverent, devoted to reading, watchful unto prayer, anxious for brotherly love, think that I am absent from him. For can I be anything but present with him in spirit when we are of one heart and one mind? But if, which God forbid, there be among you any whisperer, or any that is double-tongued, a murmurer, or rebellious, or impatient of discipline, or restless or truant, and who is not ashamed to eat the bread of idleness, from such I should be far absent in soul even though present in body, just because he would have already set himself far from God by a distance of character and not of space.

In the meanwhile, brethren, until I come, serve the Lord in fear, that in Him being delivered from the hand of your enemies you may serve Him without fear. Serve Him in hope, for He is faithful that promised; serve Him by good works, for He is bountiful to reward. To say nothing else, He rightly claims this life of ours as His own, because He laid down His own to obtain it. Let none, therefore, live to himself, but to Him who died for him. For whom can I more justly live than for Him whose death was my life? for whom with more profit to myself than for Him who promises eternal life? for whom under a greater necessity than for Him who threatens me with everlasting flames? But I serve Him willingly, because love gives liberty. To this I exhort my children. Serve Him in that love which casteth out fear, which feels no labours, seeks for no reward, thinks of no merit, and yet is more urgent than all. No terror is so powerful, no rewards so inviting, no righteousness so exacting. May it join me to you never to be divided, may it also bring me before you, especially at your hours of prayer, my brethren, dearly beloved and greatly longed for.

St. Bernard of
Clairvaux, *To His Monks
of Clairvaux.*

Additional Biblical Reflections: Psalm 122:1; 1 Corinthians 1:10; 1 Peter 3:8.

Prayer

Lord, even as your body cannot be divided against itself, let your Church, your body by virtue of being your Bride and one-in-flesh with you, be spared of fruitless divisions. Let us bear with one another charitably, placing the best construction on others' words and actions so that in all things, we might be built up in your image. Amen.

DAY 29

To ponder our future hope is not to dwell in the clouds, absent of the present. Rather, a future-oriented joy invades the present in such a way where even things that might cause us to despair are not devoid of joy in God's presence. With many biblical citations, St. Bernard reminds us to fix our eyes on the hope of God's promises.

Meditations from St. Bernard

But it will be well to note what class of people takes comfort in the thought of God. Surely not that perverse and crooked generation to whom it was said, 'Woe unto you that are rich; for ye have received your consolation' (Luke 6.24). Rather, those who can say with truth, 'My soul refuseth comfort' (Ps. 77.2). For it is meet that those who are not satisfied by the present should be sustained by the thought of the future, and that the contemplation of eternal happiness should solace those who scorn to drink from the river of transitory joys. That is the generation of them that seek the Lord, even of them that seek, not their own, but the face of the God of Jacob. To them that long for the presence of the living God, the thought of Him is sweetest itself: but there is no satiety, rather an ever-increasing appetite, even as the Scripture bears witness, 'they that eat me shall yet be hungry' (Ecclus. 24.21); and if the one an-hungred spake, 'When I awake up after Thy likeness, I shall be satisfied with it.' Yea, blessed even now are they which do hunger and thirst after righteousness, for they, and they only, shall be filled. Woe to you, wicked and perverse generation; woe to you, foolish and abandoned people, who hate Christ's memory, and dread His second Advent! Well may you fear, who will not now seek deliverance from the snare of the hunter; because 'they that will be rich fall into temptation and a snare, and into many foolish and hurtful lusts' (I Tim. 6.9). In that day we shall not escape the dreadful sentence of condemnation, 'Depart from Me, ye cursed, into everlasting fire' (Matt. 25.41). O dreadful sentence indeed, O hard saying! How much harder to bear than that other saying which we repeat daily in church, in memory of the Passion: 'Whoso eateth My flesh and drinketh My blood hath eternal life' (John 6.54). That signifies, whoso honors My death and after My example mortifies his members which are upon the earth (Col. 3.5) shall have eternal life, even as the apostle says, 'If we suffer, we shall also reign with Him' (II Tim. 2.12). And yet many even today recoil from these words and go away, saying by their action if not with their lips, 'This is a hard saying; who can hear it?' (John 6.60). 'A generation that set not their heart aright, and whose spirit cleaveth not steadfastly unto God' (Ps. 78.8), but chooseth rather to trust in uncertain riches, it is disturbed at the very name of the Cross, and counts the memory of the Passion intolerable. How can such sustain the burden of that fearful sentence, 'Depart from Me, ye cursed, into everlasting fire, prepared for the devil and his angels'? 'On whomsoever that stone shall fall it will grind him to powder' (Luke 20.18); but 'the generation of the faithful shall be blessed' (Ps. 112.2), since, like the apostle, they labor that whether present or absent they may be accepted of the Lord (II Cor. 5.9). At the last day they too shall hear the Judge pronounce their award, 'Come, ye blessed of My Father, inherit the kingdom prepared for you from the foundation of the world' (Matt. 25.34).

St. Bernard of Clairvaux. *On Loving God*, Ch. 4.

Additional Biblical Reflections: Jeremiah 29:11; Matthew 6:33; James 4:12-15.

Prayer

Lord, by securing our future, you have also redeemed our present and past. Let us not live with a hope that is devoid of impact on the future but let your hope change our lives here and now, so we might see today not as a time we must merely endure but as the beginning of our lives in your eternity. In Jesus's name. Amen.

DAY 30

While we have cause to lament in this world, our lament is not merely on account of our sufferings. Rather, as the Bridegroom nears, and we are His Bridegroom, we lament for those who do not know the coming joy that consumes our lives. We lament not because we suffer, for we know that our suffering is temporary, but for those whose futures know only wrath.

Meditations from St. Bernard

In that day those who set not their hearts aright will feel, too late, how easy is Christ's yoke, to which they would not bend their necks and how light His burden, in comparison with the pains they must then endure. O wretched slaves of Mammon, you cannot glory in the Cross of our Lord Jesus Christ while you trust in treasures laid up on earth: you cannot taste and see how gracious the Lord is, while you are hungering for gold. If you have not rejoiced at the thought of His coming, that day will be indeed a day of wrath to you.

But the believing soul longs and faints for God; she rests sweetly in the contemplation of Him. She glories in the reproach of the Cross, until the glory of His face shall be revealed. Like the Bride, the dove of Christ, that is covered with silver wings (Ps. 68.13), white with innocence and purity, she reposes in the thought of Thine abundant kindness, Lord Jesus; and above all she longs for that day when in the joyful splendor of Thy saints, gleaming with the radiance of the Beatific Vision, her feathers shall be like gold, resplendent with the joy of Thy countenance.

Rightly then may she exult, 'His left hand is under my head and His right hand doth embrace me.' The left hand signifies the memory of that matchless love, which moved Him to lay down His life for His friends; and the right hand is the Beatific Vision which He hath promised to His own, and the delight they have in His presence. The Psalmist sings rapturously, 'At Thy right hand there is pleasure for evermore' (Ps. 16.11): so we are warranted in explaining the right hand as that divine and deifying joy of His presence.

Rightly too is that wondrous and ever-memorable love symbolized as His left hand, upon which the Bride rests her head until iniquity be done away: for He sustains the purpose of her mind, lest it should be turned aside to earthly, carnal desires. For the flesh wars against the spirit: 'The corruptible body presseth down the soul, and the earthly tabernacle weigheth down the mind that museth upon many things' (Wisdom 9.15). What could result from the contemplation of compassion so marvelous and so undeserved, favor so free and so well attested, kindness so unexpected, clemency so unconquerable, grace so amazing except that the soul should withdraw from all sinful affections, reject all that is inconsistent with God's love, and yield herself wholly to heavenly things? No wonder is it that the Bride, moved by the perfume of these unctions, runs swiftly, all on fire with love, yet reckons herself as loving all too little in return for the Bridegroom's love. And rightly, since it is no great matter that a little dust should be all consumed with love of that Majesty which loved her first and which revealed itself as wholly bent on saving her. For 'God so loved the world that He gave His only-begotten Son, that whosoever believeth in Him should not perish but have everlasting life' (John 3.16). This sets forth the Father's love. But 'He hath poured out His soul unto death,' was written of the Son (Isa. 53.12). And of the Holy Spirit it is said, 'The Comforter which is the Holy Ghost whom the Father will send in My name, He shall teach you all things, and bring all things to your remembrance, whatsoever I have said unto you' (John 14.26). It is plain, therefore, that God loves us, and loves us with all

His heart; for the Holy Trinity altogether loves us, if we may venture so to speak of the infinite and incomprehensible Godhead who is essentially one.

St. Bernard of
Clairvaux. *On Loving
God*, Ch. 4.

Additional Biblical Reflections: Matthew 25:1-13; 2 Corinthians 11:2; Revelation 19:7.

Prayer

We wait for you, Lord, as a bride longing for the coming of her bridegroom. May we long for you with holy eyes, always alert and ready, so, should you reappear, we will be ready to embrace you covered by the grace merited by you on the cross. Wash us clean of our iniquities, as a bride washed for her bridegroom so that we might be pleasing to you in every way. In His name. Amen.

www.ingramcontent.com/pod-product-compliance
Lightning Source LLC
Chambersburg PA
CBHW071633040426
42452CB00009B/1600